T0099831

Why Smart Men Marry Smart Women

Christine B. Whelan

Simon & Schuster
NEW YORK LONDON TORONTO SYDNEY

SIMON & SCHUSTER
Rockefeller Center
1230 Avenue of the Americas
New York, NY 10020

SWANS, Strong Women Achievers No Spouse and
SWANS (Strong Women Achievers No Spouse) are
trademarks of Christine B. Whelan used herein under license.

For information about special discounts for bulk purchases,
please contact Simon & Schuster Special Sales:
1-800-456-6798 or business@simonandschuster.com

Names and characteristics of certain individuals described
in this book have been changed.

DESIGNED BY PAUL DIPPOLITO

Manufactured in the United States of America

1   3   5   7   9   10   8   6   4   2

The author gratefully acknowledges permission from the
following source to reprint material in their control: illustration
on p. viii © Barbara McGregor / www.artscouncilinc.com

Library of Congress Control Number 2006050563

ISBN-13: 978-1-4516-4341-1

For Peter, with love

Contents